Painted Chairs for Tiny Tots

Short and tall, *but they're all small*—here are 11 adorable chairs and stools to paint for kids. Designed by seven decorative artists, there's something to delight every munchkin in your life. Paint bears, bunnies, butterflies, and bugs on unfinished chairs found at the craft store or add colorful flowers, dots, and stripes to the old family rocker. Choose a theme to match your child's room from Noah's soft pastel animals for baby to vibrant primary-colored hand-prints for the preschooler. Then personalize any chair with your child's name using the alphabet on page 11. With the projects and ideas in this book you can create truly special chairs that will be treasured for generations.

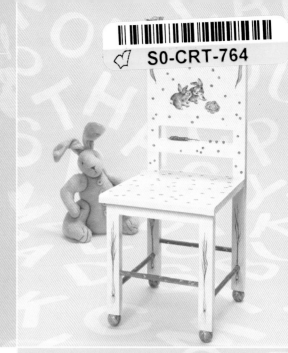

Contents

General Instructions

Materials

You'll find specific materials lists printed alongside the project instructions. Before getting started, you'll also need to gather the following general supplies:

- Disposable palette paper (sold in pads) for laying out paints. Substitute with freezer paper, foam meat trays, or plastic lids. An artist's wet palette is useful for keeping paints moist for a longer period of time.

- Water container, glass jar, or commercial brush basin

- Various grades of sandpaper and lint-free cloth or tack cloth

- Tracing paper and a fine-tip permanent black pen or pencil

- Transfer paper (sometimes called graphite paper) and pencil, dry ballpoint pen, or stylus

- Paint mixing tool: palette knife, or plastic or wood (popsicle) stick

- Paper towels for absorbing water from brushes and for general cleanup

- Ruler, white art eraser

Getting Started

The projects in this book are created by seven different artists. Methods for preparing or finishing projects may vary depending on their personal preferences. As you experiment with different paints and mediums, you'll discover your favorite methods.

Paints

The artists use bottled, non-toxic water-based acrylic paints from several different manufacturers. They are available at your local craft or hobby store, by mail order, or online. If your craft supplier does not have the specific brand listed, just substitute with similar colors from another manufacturer.

Acrylic paints dry relatively quickly and clean up with soap and water. In most instances paint colors are used straight from the bottle, however, artists sometimes specify colors that require mixing or thinning with water. A plus symbol (+) between color names in the text indicates the colors should be mixed. Use a palette knife for mixing; start with the lighter color then gradually add the darker color to get the desired hue.

Brushes

The brushes are listed by size and style (#2 flat, #4 round, etc.) and may also include brand information. Using the correct size and style will help you achieve the desired effect, but if a particular brand is not readily available, again, just substitute with something similar. It's important to take good care of brushes, so they'll last a long while. Rinse often during use, but don't let them sit in a water container for long periods of time. After use, clean thoroughly with soap and water (or brush cleaner), working the soap into the bristles. Always rinse well. Store dry brushes flat or with handles down.

Surfaces

You'll find a variety of surfaces at craft and department stores or online. For most projects it's not necessary to use the exact surface shown in the model. The designs can be adapted to practically any surface you like. Use your imagination to visualize the designs on different surfaces. Since a project surface may vary somewhat in size from piece to piece, it may be necessary to adjust the pattern slightly to fit your surface.

Preparation

Be sure to complete this important step before applying your design. Individual project instructions may include special methods of preparation. In general, prepare a wood surface by first filling any holes or dents with wood filler. Sand the entire piece with medium-grit sandpaper and remove any dust. Apply a coat of wood sealer and allow to dry thoroughly. Sand with

fine-grit sandpaper and wipe clean.

For most projects, apply an overall basecoat or background color. To keep the surface as smooth and even as possible, use a large flat brush and apply several light coats rather than one heavy one. It may take 2–3 coats for good coverage. Be sure to let each coat dry before adding another.

Patterns

Patterns are printed full-size. To transfer, first trace the pattern onto transparent tracing paper using a fine-tip, permanent black pen or pencil. Trace as accurately as possible. Be sure any basecoated areas are dry before you begin to transfer the pattern or the lines may be difficult to remove later (a hair dryer can speed up the drying time). Tape the pattern to the surface in the desired position, then slip a piece of transfer or graphite paper underneath, making sure you have the graphite side down.

Use gray transfer paper for projects with light-colored backgrounds and white transfer paper (or white chalk) for projects with dark backgrounds. Trace over the design using a pencil, inkless pen, or small end of a stylus. Apply with light pressure to avoid leaving indentations on the surface and to keep lines light.

In some cases you may need to transfer a design in several steps, starting with the main areas of the design then later adding detail lines.

When your project is finished, remove tracing lines with a white art eraser, damp cotton swab, or odorless turpentine on a soft cloth.

Finishing

After removing any visible transfer lines, follow the artist's instructions for finishing the project. For varnishing, water-based products are recommended for their compatibility with the water-based acrylic paints, quick drying time, and minimal odor. Be sure to follow the manufacturer's instructions.

Painting Terms

Basecoat: Paint the entire piece with one color (see preparation above) or apply background colors to specific areas of the design.

Float/Sideload: This is a common technique used for shading and highlighting. Moisten a flat brush in water and gently blot out the excess moisture on a paper towel. Dip the corner in a puddle of paint then stroke back and forth in a uniform motion on your palette. The color will bleed across the brush, leaving strong color on one side and fading to plain water on the other side.

Doubleload: With this technique you load two colors on the brush at once, allowing you to shade and highlight with one stroke. To doubleload, dip

one corner of a flat brush in your first color, then dip the other corner in a different color; the two colors should meet in the middle. On your palette, stroke the brush back and forth on both sides to blend.

Drybrush: For this method of highlighting or adding texture, start with a dry brush and load the color sparingly. Wipe the brush with a clean paper towel, leaving only a small amount of paint on the bristles. Apply the color using short, sweeping strokes.

Stipple/Pounce: Load the brush sparingly and apply the color to the surface in an up-and-down tapping motion. This leaves an irregular pattern of color that covers the base color only partially.

Spatter/Flyspeck: Use an old toothbrush to add flecks of color to the design. Thin paint with water then dip the toothbrush into the paint. Pull the bristles back using your thumb, fingernail, or a palette knife to fling a spray of color. Practice first on some newspaper to test your aim, the range of spray, and thickness of coverage.

Wash, Glaze, or Tint: To shade, highlight, or add interest to a design, apply a transparent layer of color using a scant amount of paint or thinning it slightly with water or extender.

Samantha's Convertible

By Barbara Baatz Hillman

Palette

Delta Ceramcoat Acrylics

Amethyst	Magenta
Apple Green	Maple Sugar Tan
Blue Jay	Oasis Green
Calypso Orange	Ocean Reef Blue
Dark Foliage Green	Olive Yellow
Deep Lilac	Pumpkin
Fuchsia	Putty
GP Purple	Salem Green
Laguna Blue	Tangerine
Light Foliage Green	Tomato Spice
Light Ivory	Turquoise
Lisa Pink	Village Green

Brushes

Loew-Cornell, Inc.
¾", 1½" wash: Series 7550C
#6, 10, 12 shaders: Series 7300C
#1, 2 liners: Series 7350C
#2, 4, 6, 8 filberts: Series 7500C
¼", ½", ¾" angular shaders:
Series 7400C

Surface

Child's wood step stool/chair,
16"H x 13½"W x 12"D
(#30-418) available from *Cabin
Crafters.*

Other Supplies

Stylus
Cellophane or painter's tape
Delta Ceramcoat Gel Stain Medium
Delta Ceramcoat Satin Varnish

Sources

Refer to page 44.

PREPARATION & BASECOATS

Note: When painting each chair section, tape off any connecting parts of the chair with cellophane or painter's tape to avoid getting unwanted paint on them.

1. Please read carefully the General Instructions on pages 2–3 before starting and prepare the wood surface as instructed. Project pattern is on the center insert.

2. Basecoat the top, bottom, and sides of the seat and foot/backrest and also the entire moveable sides with Putty. Basecoat the inside and outside of the stationary sides with Maple Sugar Tan.

3. Paint the two connecting dowels with Blue Jay.

4. On the inside and outside of the stationary sides, paint stripes going from the top to bottom approximately ½" apart, using a #12 shader and Putty. These are not supposed to look perfect—this is a fun project!

5. On the moveable sides, using a #10 shader and Maple Sugar Tan, paint vertical stripes the length of the sides and about a brush width apart. When dry, create a plaid look by painting horizontal stripes in the same way. In each of the resulting light-colored squares, paint a Lisa Pink dot using the #4 filbert brush.

6. With a liner, paint an undulating line around the edges of all sections (refer to photo).

SEAT

Checkered Border

1. Use a ruler and pencil to mark a 1" line all around the seat top. Paint the resulting border with Light Ivory. Mix *Gel Stain Medium* + Blue Jay (2:1) and glaze around the border—darker toward the interior, lighter toward the edge. Dry completely.

2. Divide borders in half lengthwise

4

Flip the backrest down on this clever little chair and it becomes a handy step stool for keeping things in reach.

and mark off ½" squares. Paint every other square Deep Lilac with one stroke of the #12 shader. When dry, paint a slightly smaller square in the middle of each Deep Lilac square with GP Purple. When the checkered border is completely dry, tape it off.

Center Background Design

1. For the background, add enough water to Maple Sugar Tan to thin well, then, using a ¾" wash brush, paint light vertical stripes approximately ½" apart through the center Putty section. Dry thoroughly.

2. Remove the tape from the checkered border and paint a thin Ocean Reef Blue line between the checkered and striped sections.

3. Transfer the pattern for the seat floral motif to the center section.

Vines, Stems, Sepals, & Leaves

1. Paint the curled-end vines, as well as the short stems and sepals on the flowers with Olive Yellow.
2. Basecoat the blue leaves with Oasis Green and the green leaves with Light Foliage Green.
3. Shade around the base, down both sides of the center vein, and wherever the leaf is overlapped by another leaf or flower. Use Salem Green on the blue leaves and Dark Foliage Green on the green leaves.
4. Paint the veins on the blue leaves with Village Green and on the green leaves with Apple Green.

FLOWERS

Note: Paint flowers furthest from the center first, then work toward center.

Pink Roses

1. Basecoat the roses with Lisa Pink, then paint over the rose center with Tangerine.
2. Shade the Tangerine with Tomato Spice, then add small dots using the stylus.
3. Shade the petals with Fuchsia. (Refer to photo and worksheet for placement.)
4. Highlight the top edge of each petal with Light Ivory.

Small Fuchsia Circle Flowers

1. Basecoat the three flower circles in the group with Fuchsia.
2. Shade the largest of the three with Magenta and add a small Magenta center.
3. Highlight around the bottom edge of the Magenta center with Lisa Pink, and add a Lisa Pink center to the two smaller circles.

Blue Flowers

1. Basecoat the outside of the flowers with Blue Jay and the center with Calypso Orange.
2. Shade the base of the flower with Ocean Reef Blue and the center with Pumpkin.
3. Add Tangerine dots to the center with the stylus.

Purple/Turquoise Flowers

1. Basecoat the outside of the flower with GP Purple and the center with Turquoise.
2. Shade the purple with Deep Lilac and the Turquoise center with Laguna Blue.
3. Deepen the purple shading, where it comes from behind the large center flower, with Amethyst.
4. Paint the spiral in the center with Deep Lilac.

Small Purple Circle Flowers

1. Paint the two largest circles with GP Purple and the smallest circle with Deep Lilac.
2. Shade the largest circle with Deep Lilac, then add a Deep Lilac center to the two smaller circles.

Pink & Orange Circle Flowers

1. Basecoat the largest circle with Lisa Pink with a Tangerine center. Paint the middle circle Pumpkin and the smallest circle Calypso Orange.
2. Shade the pink circle with Fuchsia. Add a Calypso Orange center to the middle circle.
3. On the pink circle, paint a ring between the pink and the orange and a small oval in the center of the orange with Ocean Reef Blue.

Large Center Flower

1. Basecoat the petals with Lisa Pink, the rings with Ocean Reef Blue and Calypso Orange, and the center with Pumpkin.
2. Shade all around each petal with Fuchsia and shade around the Pumpkin center with Tangerine.
3. Using Magenta, paint a thin line between each petal and three short lines within each petal from the base toward the tip. Add small dots all

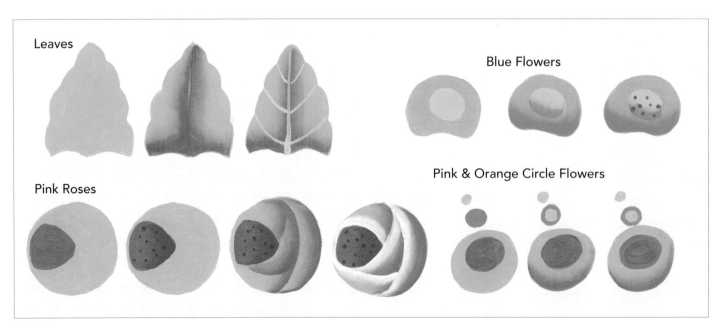

Leaves

Blue Flowers

Pink Roses

Pink & Orange Circle Flowers

around the Calypso Orange ring with Tangerine and paint a Calypso Orange spot in the Pumpkin center.
4. Highlight the petals between the Magenta lines with Light Ivory.

FOOT/BACKREST

Note: Most of the flowers in the foot/backrest are also in the seat design and should be painted with the same colors and in the same manner except as instructed below. On the backrest, because of the thickness of the side sections, there will only be room for one row of checks on the sides. This will make the center section slightly smaller, so the curled vines will go to the very edges of the checkered border.

FLOWERS

Small Turquoise Spiral Circles

1. Paint the circles with Turquoise and shade with Laguna Blue.
2. Paint a spiral in the largest circle and add a tiny center in the smaller circle with Deep Lilac.

Center Flower

1. Paint the main flower Lisa Pink with a Tangerine center.
2. Shade around the outside of the flower with Fuchsia and shade the center with Tomato Spice.
3. Highlight the flower with Light Ivory and dot the center with Tomato Spice.

FINISHING

1. Allow to dry thoroughly then erase any transfer lines that may be remaining.
2. Give the entire chair two coats of satin varnish with a couple of extra coats on the seat and foot/backrest since these will get the most wear.

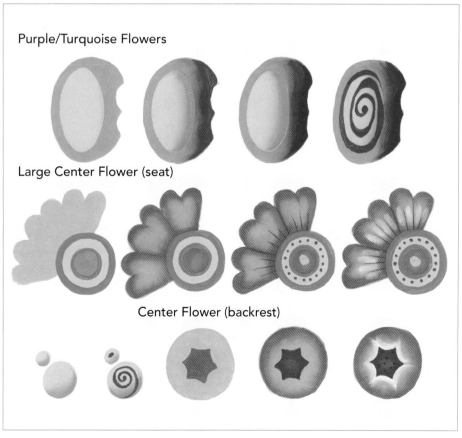

Purple/Turquoise Flowers

Large Center Flower (seat)

Center Flower (backrest)

Stamp Your Hands & Feet

By Linda Gillum

Palette

DecoArt Americana Acrylics
Avocado
Lamp Black
Lavender
Olive Green
Purple
Snow White
Taffy Cream
True Blue
True Red

Brushes

Loew-Cornell, Inc.
1" glaze/wash: Series 7550
¼" angular shader: Series 7400
#4, 8 rounds: Series 7000
#1 liner: Series 7350

Surface

Wood chair: 36"H x 12"W x 10½"D
Wood stool with rectangular top:
    7¼"H x 10¾"W x 9"D
Both available at crafts stores.

Other Supplies

DecoArt Multi-Purpose Sealer
Spray or brush-on varnish

Sources

Refer to page 44.

PREPARATION

1. Please read carefully the General Instructions on pages 2-3 before starting this project. Patterns are on page 10.
2. Sand the chair and stool, fill in holes with wood putty, and seal with multi-purpose sealer.

PAINTING THE DESIGN
Chair

1. Measure 1½" from the bottom of the top backrest bar and draw a horizontal line to mark off the checked area. Using a 1" wash brush and Snow White, fill in this area. When dry, draw two more horizontal lines spaced ½" apart then draw verticals lines spaced ½" apart to create the three rows of checks. Leaving one white check at the left side of the bottom row, fill in alternate checks using Lamp Black and the ¼" angular brush. Let dry then repeat with the rows above, starting the middle row with black and the top row again with white. Touch up, if needed, using the liner brush.
2. Paint the seat supports on all four sides of the chair with Snow White. For the striped area below the seat front, first basecoat using the 1" wash and Snow White. Draw vertical lines spaced ½" apart. Use the ¼" angular brush and Lamp Black to fill in stripes starting at the left with a black stripe.
3. Mark a line 3" below the top of each chair post for the yellow/red dot area. This should also line up with the top of the checked area. Paint with Taffy Cream continuing around the posts. Paint a ½" wide Lavender band below the Taffy Cream, followed by a 1½" wide Olive Green band.

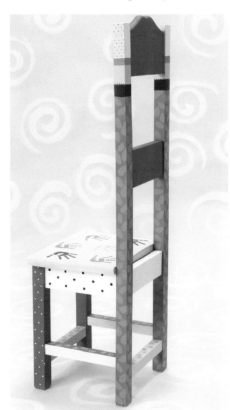

4. Paint the remaining area of the posts with True Blue. When dry add a 1" wide Lamp Black band below the Olive Green band, leaving a ⅛" strip of True Blue showing.

5. Refer to the illustration and key on page 11 for basecoat colors to paint the remaining areas of the chair.

Chair Details

1. Polka dots: Paint polka dots in horizontal rows using the end of a small, medium, or large brush depending upon the desired size of the dot. Refer to the illustration and key on page 11 for dot color. (See photo for placement and dot size.)

2. Dots: Paint a row of Taffy Cream medium-sized dots spaced ⅛" apart on top of the ⅛" True Blue strip on the posts.

3. Leaves: Paint assorted leaf shapes on True Blue areas of the posts using a light blue mix of True Blue + Snow White (1:1) and two strokes with the #8 round brush.

4. Name: Use the alphabet on page 11 to personalize the chair with your child's name. First, compose on a piece of tracing paper, enlarging letters as needed to make the name fit comfortably across the bottom bar of the backrest. Transfer to the project. Paint letters using the #4 round brush and Lamp Black.

5. Swirls: Paint loosely using the #1 liner and colors indicated in the key. Swirls are approximately ½" in diameter but should vary slightly with tails pointing in different directions for a casual look. Practice painting some on a piece of paper before painting on the wood surface.

6. Handprints: Transfer the handprint pattern six times to the chair seat, flipping the pattern to create both left and right hands. Paint as indicated in the key using the #4 round brush. Touch up, if needed, using the liner brush.

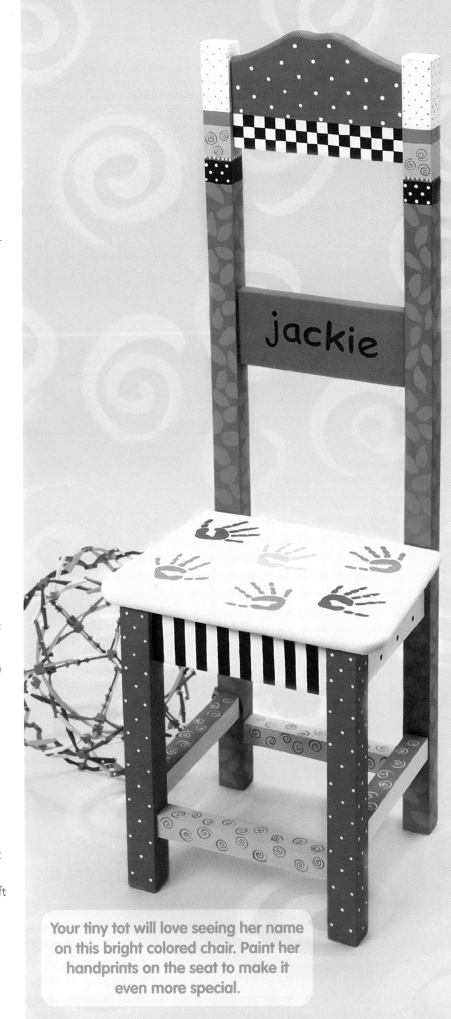

Your tiny tot will love seeing her name on this bright colored chair. Paint her handprints on the seat to make it even more special.

Footstool

1. Paint the footstool top the same as the chair seat but use the foot pattern instead of the hand pattern.
2. Paint the edges of the footstool top with ½" black and white stripes like those on the front seat support. Paint inside and outside of side supports using True Blue.
3. Paint the horizontal bar between the supports using True Red.

Footstool Details

1. On the outside of the side supports paint swirls approximately ¾" in diameter using a mix of True Blue + Snow White (1:1).
2. Use the end of a large brush and Snow Whte to add three horizontal rows of polka dots on both sides of the red support bar.

FINISHING

1. Apply 2–3 coats of satin spray or brush-on varnish to protect the painting.

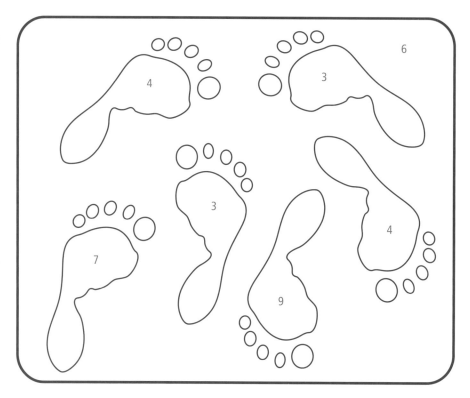

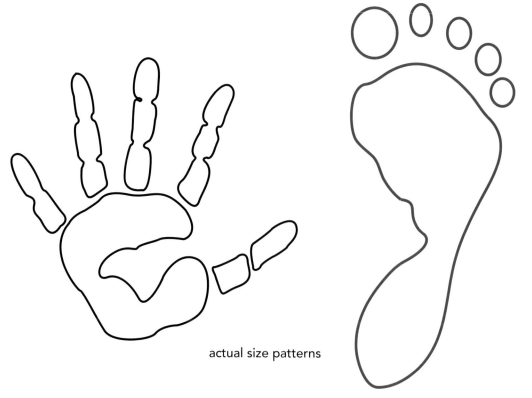

actual size patterns

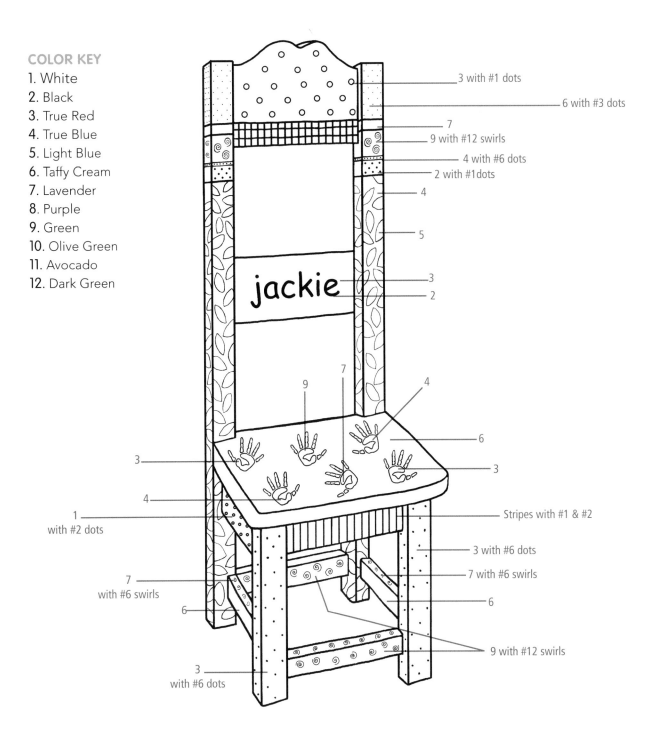

COLOR KEY
1. White
2. Black
3. True Red
4. True Blue
5. Light Blue
6. Taffy Cream
7. Lavender
8. Purple
9. Green
10. Olive Green
11. Avocado
12. Dark Green

3 with #1 dots

6 with #3 dots

7

9 with #12 swirls

4 with #6 dots

2 with #1dots

4

5

3

2

jackie

9

7

4

6

3

3

4

1
with #2 dots

Stripes with #1 & #2

3 with #6 dots

7 with #6 swirls

7
with #6 swirls

6

6

9 with #12 swirls

3
with #6 dots

abcdefghijklm
nopqrstuvwxyz

11

Eat Your Veggies!

By Peggy Harris

Palette

FolkArt Artists' Pigments
Fawn
Hauser Green Light
Hauser Green Medium
Medium Yellow
Pure Black
Raw Umber
Red Light
Titanium White
Warm White

Brushes

Silver Brush, Ltd. Ruby Satin
#4 traditional bright (stiff flat): Series 2502S
Silver Brush, Ltd. Golden Natural
1" square wash: Series 2008S
#2 shader (soft flat): Series 2002S
5/0 round: Series 2000S
Silver Brush, Ltd. Ultra Mini
#2 designer round: Series 2431S
12/0 angle (optional): Series 2404S
Silver Brush, Ltd. Wee Mop
⅛" or ³⁄₁₆" mop: Series 5319S
Peggy's Ultimate Varnish Brush
1" oval varnish: Series 2303S
Brushes available through
www.peggyharris.com.

Surface

Child's chair, 27"H x 11"W x 11"D
(#100864) available from
Cabin Crafters.

(list continued on page 14)

PREPARATION

1. Please read carefully the General Instructions on pages 2-3 before starting this project. Pattern is on center insert.
2. Determine the final height of the chair once the wooden ball feet are attached. You may wish to saw one or two inches off each leg for a lower seat height. Assemble the chair, securing the back and cross rods with wood glue. Let cure.
3. Fill any imperfections in the wood with wood filler. Let dry thoroughly. Lightly sand the chair. Wipe clean with a tack cloth. Seal the chair and wooden balls with white acrylic primer. Dry and re-sand. Remove dust with a tack cloth.
4. Opaquely basecoat all surfaces of the chair with a 1" wash brush and Warm White. Basecoat the small wooden balls with Hauser Green Medium. Basecoat large balls with Hauser Green Light. When dry, generously spray all surfaces with matte acrylic spray. Dry well.
5. Carefully trace the design and transfer with gray transfer paper. The transferred design should be as pale as possible. Lighten with a kneaded eraser, if necessary.

ARTIST'S NOTES

1. The slick surface created by spraying the base painted chair provides effortless clean up of stray paint. If you prefer, apply a light coat of varnish rather than spraying the surface.
2. Use a clean, wet, stiff bright brush or wet cotton swabs as "erasers" to sharpen shapes or lift out mistakes.
3. Veggies are best painted with whichever brush best fits the space and a variety of greens brush mixed as you work from Hauser Green Medium, Hauser Green Light, Titanium White, and Medium Yellow (optional).
4. Mop brushes must be kept dry to work effectively. Do not clean mops in water until you have finished painting.
5. Use gel medium to extend the open time and/or make paint transparent. A slick of gel under paint aids blending. Add gel to paint to make transparent glazes of color to adjust underpinning.
6. Force dry gel/paint with a dryer before adding successive layers of gel and paint to prevent surprise lifting of paint that appears dry.
7. A "barrier" coat of matte acrylic spray may be applied at any interval. This allows for foolproof and fearless application of more layers.

PAINTING PROCEDURE

Lettering

1. Carefully paint the transferred lettering with Hauser Green Light. Use a #2 soft shader for broader strokes and a 5/0 round brush for thin strokes.
2. Sharpen edges with a #2 stiff bright brush "eraser."

Green Beans

1. Paint the beans with a #2 soft shader and brush mixes of Hauser Green Medium or Hauser Green Light lightened with Titanium White.
2. Paint one side of the beans darker than the other.

Bunnies

1. With a fully loaded 5/0 round brush, paint beady Pure Black eyes.

A simple palette and easy, repeated pattern make veggies more fun to paint than to eat.

VEGGIES

(list continued from page 12)

Other Supplies

Six 1" wooden balls (flat on bottom)
Ten ¼" wooden balls
One paper/wire twist-tie
Two large artificial yellow roses with
    leaves
Wood glue
Super Glue Gel
Folk Art
    Blending Gel Medium
    ClearCote Matte Acrylic Sealer
        (spray)
J.W., Etc.
    Wood Filler
    UnderCover white acrylic primer
    Right-Step Satin Varnish
    Painter's Finishing Wax
    #0000 white synthetic steel
        wool pad
Heat-It Craft Tool (or hair dryer)
Masterson Sta-Wet Handy Palette
Super fine wet/dry sandpaper
    or sanding film
Kneaded eraser
Cotton swabs

Sources

Refer to page 44.

2. With the same brush and inky Raw Umber, mark the location of the tiny noses and toe lines.

3. Brush mix Titanium White + Red Light and blush the muzzles with a 12/0 angular brush. Force dry with a dryer.

4. Apply a slick of gel to a bunny with a soft shader. With a scant amount of Fawn on the tip of a clean, dry ⅛" or ³⁄₁₆" mop, gently tap color into the darkest shadow areas of a bunny.

5. Scrub the brush clean on a paper towel. With the clean brush, proceed to blend the color into surrounding areas. The paint will become more transparent as you work away from the darkest shadows. Avoid the highlight areas. Highlights are formed automatically as the white base paint shows through the painting.

6. Intensify color slowly, force drying the painting with a dryer between layers of gel/paint. You may spray the painting with matte acrylic spray before proceeding with deepest shading.

7. Once you are satisfied with the intensity of the Fawn color, use the same technique, but with a #2 soft shader, to add touches of Raw Umber in the deepest shadow areas of the fur. The underlying gel will make the Raw Umber transparent, allowing the fuzzy texture of the Fawn fur to show through.

VEGGIES

Cabbage

1. Using a 12/0 angular and 5/0 round

brush, paint the cabbage with brush mixed greens of Hauser Green Light + Titanium White.

2. Shade the deepest shadows with Hauser Green Medium.

Peas

1. Use a 12/0 angular and/or a 5/0 round brush and Hauser Green Medium + Hauser Green Light to randomly paint peas over the chair back.

2. While the paint is still wet, stir a bit of Hauser Green Light + Titanium White into the center of each pea to create a slight highlight.

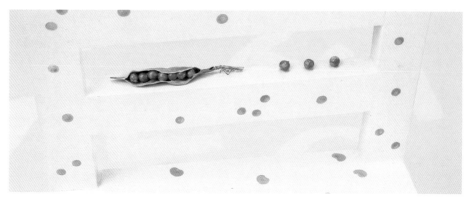

1. Tap in Fawn fur with a ⅛" mop over a slick of gel medium. Dry.

Base the cabbage with brush mixed greens.

2. Tap in another layer of Fawn fur over a slick of gel medium. Dry.

Shade the cabbage with Hauser Green Medium.

3. Shade the bunnies with a #2 shader and Raw Umber.

Add cabbage veins using T itanium White and a #2 de-signer round.

4. Freehand limas about the chair seat and peas about the chair back.

5. Freehand asparagus dowels.

Limas

1. With a #2 soft shader and/or a 12/0 angular and Hauser Green Light + Titanium White, randomly freehand lima beans on the chair seat.
2. When dry, shade the limas with Hauser Green Medium and a 12/0 angular.

Green Onions

1. Using the #2 designer round or the #2 soft shader and brush mixing as you work, paint the onions with various mixes of Hauser Green Medium or Hauser Green Light, Titanium White, and Medium Yellow (optional).
2. Shade one side of the bulb with Fawn. Highlight the center of the bulb with Titanium White.

Brussel Sprouts Feet

1. Attach the basecoated wooden balls to each foot with wood glue.
2. Once cured, use brush mixed lighter greens and a #2 soft shader to simulate leaves.
3. Paint pale squiggly veins with a designer round brush.

Asparagus Dowels

1. Undercoat the dowels with a 1" wash brush and Hauser Green Light. Let dry.
2. Freehand the details of the asparagus tops and stems with brush mixed Hauser Green Light + Titanium White + touch Medium Yellow.

Cabbage Finials

1. Glue the basecoated balls to the top center of each post of the chair back.
2. Remove several petals from each artificial rose bud. Trim the lower edge of each petal in a semicircle. Position around the wooden finial balls to determine the height of each petal.
3. Color the petals with very watery Hauser Green Medium + Titanium White + touch Medium Yellow. Brush-

mix the paint as you work for a variance of color. Darkest color should be at the base of each petal. Let dry.
4. Reposition the petal "leaves" around the wooden finials. Overlap the leaves as you attach them to the ball and to each other with *Super Glue Gel*. Hold in place until each leaf is firmly adhered.
5. Add squiggly veins and leaf edges to the center of each cabbage (the wooden ball) with a designer round brush and Hauser Green Light + Titanium White + Medium Yellow (optional). Brush mix as you work to vary the color.

Pea Pod With Peas

1. Detach a large leaf from the stem of a rose bud. Fold the leaf down the center vein. Trim the folded leaf to resemble a pea pod. Pinch the ends of the "pod" together with *Super Glue Gel*. Hold in place until the glue sets.
2. Paint the outside of the pod with

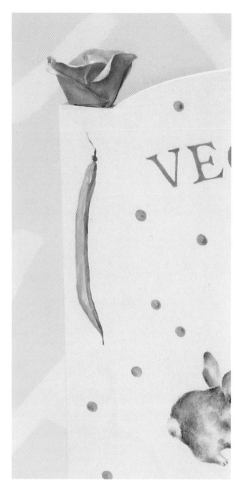

Hauser Green Medium brush mixed with a touch of Titanium White. Paint the inside of the pod with Hauser Green Light + Titanium White. Let dry.

3. Entwine a short length of wire from a twist-tie around one end to form a tendril.

4. Glue seven wooden "peas" in a row in the pod. Position and glue the pod and the three remaining peas along the cross bar.

FINISHING

1. Varnish the chair (including the cabbage finials) with multiple coats of satin varnish. Be sure to dust out the varnish brush before dipping the dry brush in the varnish. With a full load in the brush, "pool" the varnish in the middle of an area, then rapidly spread it to the edges of the area. Wipe excess varnish from the brush on a damp paper towel, then smooth the wet varnish with the brush held in a horizontal position. Use no pressure on the brush. Residual pinprick bubbles will evaporate when dry. Store the wet varnish brush in a damp paper towel between coats. This prevents diluting the varnish with water from cleaning the brush.

2. Lightly sand between later coats of varnish. Cure thoroughly.

3. Apply painter's finishing wax with a #0000 white synthetic steel wool pad. When dry, buff with a soft paper towel to enhance the varnish and bring out the beauty of the painting.

Noah's Ark, Two by Two

By Linda Gillum

Palette

DecoArt Americana Acrylics
Baby Blue
Boysenberry Pink
Buttermilk
Cadmium Yellow
Camel
Cashmere Beige
Lamp Black
Light Buttermilk
Mint Julep Green
Mocha
Peach Sherbert
Snow White
Taffy Cream
Tangerine
Victorian Blue
Wisteria

Brushes

Loew-Cornell, Inc.
1" wash: Series 7550
#4, 6 rounds: Series 7000
#1 liner: Series 7350

Surface

Oval stool: 12¾"W x 9"D x 7¾"H
Child's rocking chair: 23"H x 14"W
    x 18"D
Both available at craft stores.

Other Supplies

DecoArt Multi-Purpose Sealer
#5 Black Pigma Micron Pen
Spray or brush-on varnish

Sources

Refer to page 44.

PREPARATION

1. Please read carefully the General Instructions on pages 2-3 before starting this project. Pattern is on pages 20-21.
2. Sand the chair and stool, fill in holes with wood putty, and seal with multi-purpose sealer.

PAINTING

Stool

1. Basecoat the top of the stool Light Yellow. Basecoat the outside of the legs Light Green, the inside Light Peach, and the center support Light Blue. Paint edges of the legs Light Wisteria.
2. Transfer the design to the top of the stool.
3. Refer to the pattern and color key on pages 20-21 for painting the design.
4. Use a *#5 Black Pigma Micron Pen* to add black dots for eyes and other details and also for outlining (see photo).

Chair

1. Paint chair according to the diagram and color key on page 22.
2. Transfer the rainbow motif from the stool pattern onto the upper back of the chair and paint according to instruction drawing on page 20. Use a *#5 Black Pigma Micron Pen* to draw outlines and add details on sun face.

FINISHING

1. Apply 2–3 coats of satin spray or brush-on varnish to protect the painting.

A rainbow of soft pastel colors is the backdrop for Noah and his animal friends on this adorable chair with matching stool for baby.

COLOR KEY

1. Snow White
2. Lamp Black
3. Buttermilk
4. Light Buttermilk
5. Yellow – Cadmium Yellow + Snow White (2:1)
6. Light Yellow – Taffy Cream + Buttermilk + Snow White (1:1:4)
7. Light Yellow Orange Taffy Cream + Tangerine (1:1)
8. Medium Yellow Orange – Tangerine + Peach Sherbert (1:1)
9. Light Blue – Baby Blue + Snow White (1:3)
10. Baby Blue
11. Victorian Blue
12. Light Mint Julep Green – Mint Julep Green + Taffy Cream + Snow White (1:2:2)
13. Mint Julep Green
14. Light Peach – Peach Sherbert + Snow White (1:4)
15. Light Wisteria – Wisteria + Snow White (1:1)
16. Medium Wisteria – Wisteria + Snow White (1:1) + touch of Lamp Black
17. Dark Wisteria – Wisteria + touch of Lamp Black
18. Camel
19. Light Camel – Camel + Snow White (1:3)
20. Medium Camel – Camel + Snow White (1:2)
21. Pink – Boysenberry Pink + Snow White (1:1)
22. Light Mocha – Mocha + Snow White (1:1)
23. Mocha
24. Cashmere Beige

Noah's Ark, Two by Two
Stool Pattern

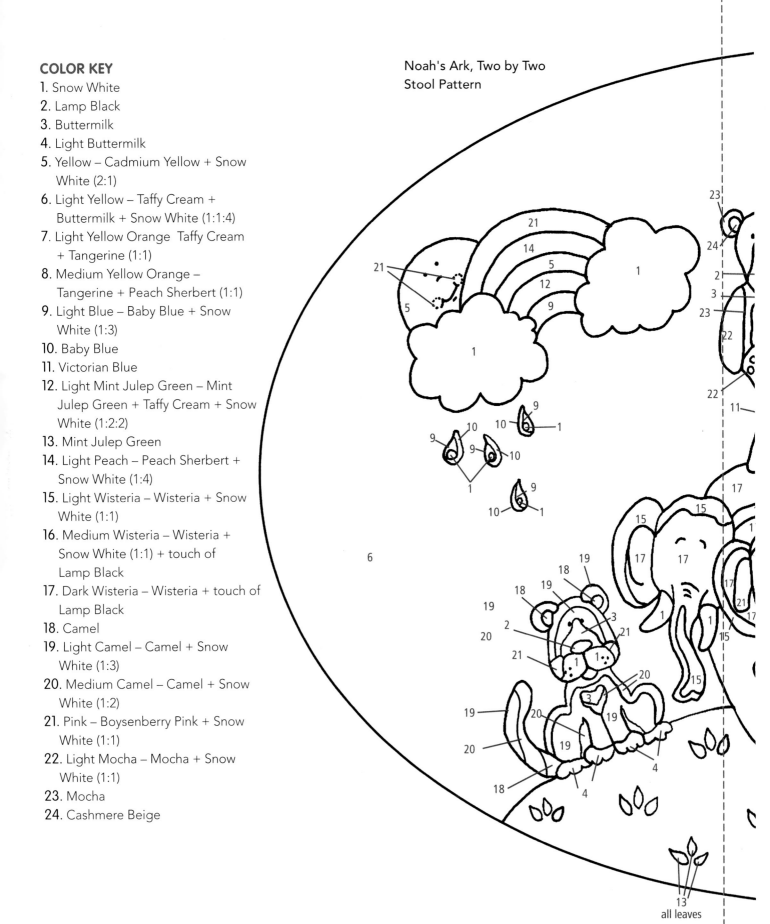

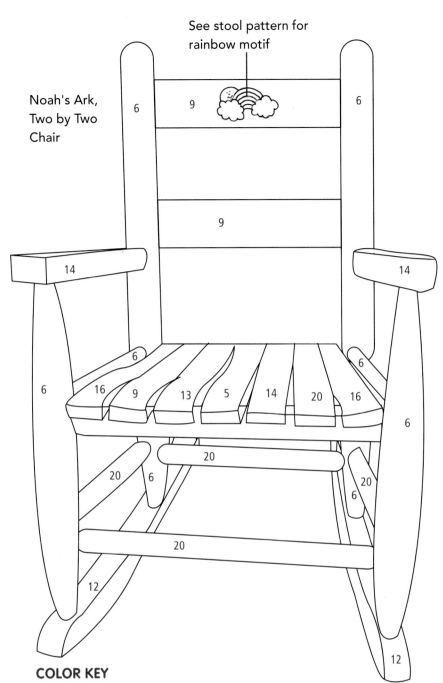

See stool pattern for rainbow motif

Noah's Ark, Two by Two Chair

COLOR KEY

5. Yellow – Cadmium Yellow + Snow White (2:1)

6. Light Yellow – Taffy Cream + Buttermilk + Snow White (1:1:4)

9. Light Blue – Baby Blue + Snow White (1:3)

12. Light Mint Julep Green – Mint Julep Green + Taffy Cream + Snow White (1:2:2)

13. Mint Julep Green

14. Light Peach – Peach Sherbert + Snow White (1:4)

16. Medium Wisteria – Wisteria + Snow White (1:1) + touch of Lamp Lamp Black

20. Medium Camel – Camel + Snow White (1:2)

Daisy Days
Swirls on Legs
1. Start with an "S" shape.

2. Start adding chains. Each swirl goes in the opposite direction of its leader.

3. Vary size and direction. More than one swirl can come off a large swirl.

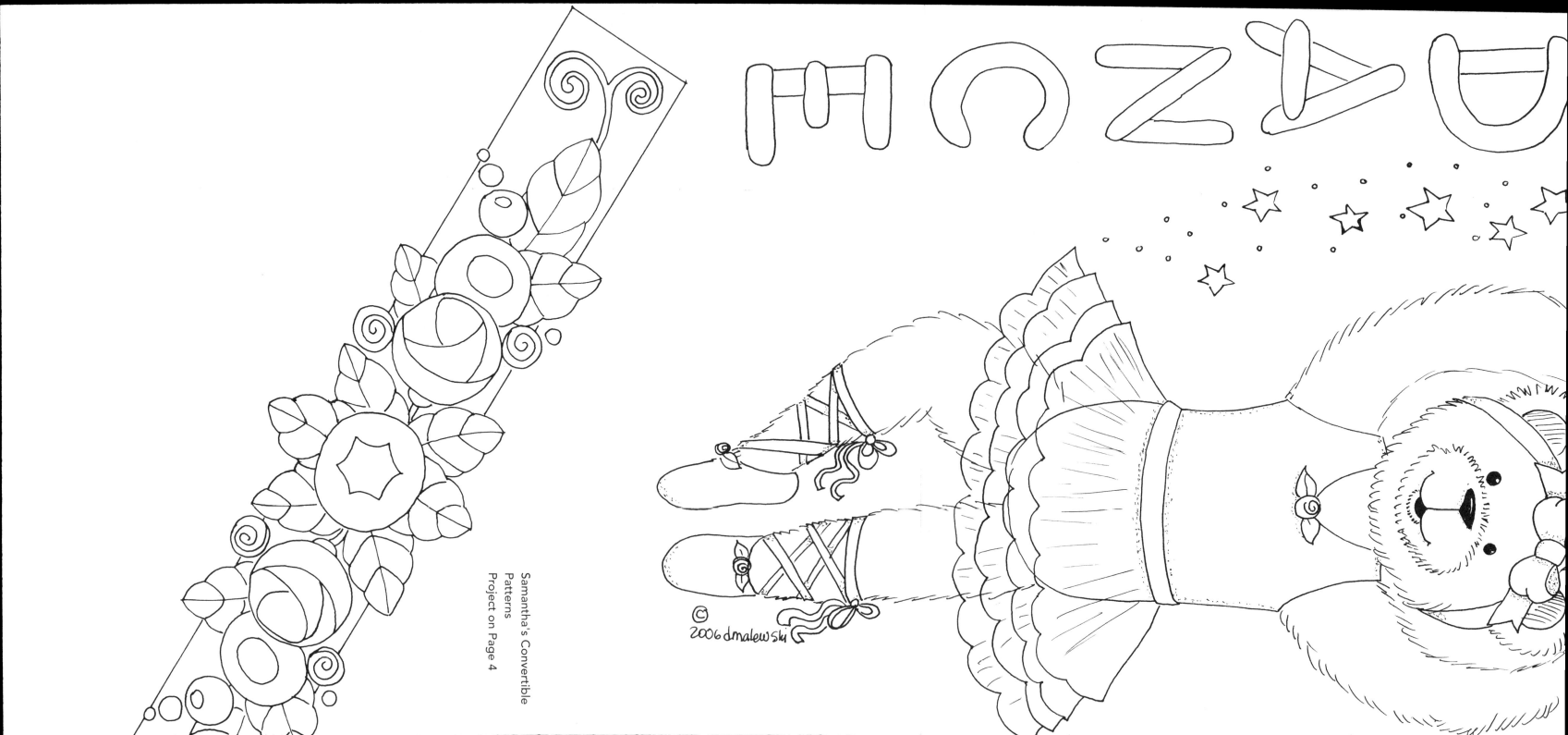

Samantha's Convertible
Patterns
Project on Page 4

© 2006 dmalewski

ABC Come Read with Me
Patterns
Project on Page 32

• left side – reverse for right side

Freehand similar pattern on dowels.

©harris '06

• right side – reverse for left side

Daisy Days Pattern
Enlarge 125% for actual size
Project on page 24

Daisy Days

By Tera Leigh

Palette

Delta Ceramcoat Acrylics
Bright Yellow
Copen Blue
Crocus Yellow
Fuchsia
Ivory
Lima Green
Magnolia White
Pthalo Blue
Pumpkin

Brushes

Robert Simmons Sapphire Brushes
#1, 2 liners: Series S51
½" filbert: Series S53
½" ¾" wash: Series S55
#10, 14 flats: Series S60
#12 round: Series S85
Robert Simmons Brushes
#10 filbert: Series T67
Simply Simmons
½" flat comb

Surface

Spindle-leg 11" round wood step
    stool available at craft stores.

Other Supplies

Delta Ceramcoat Artists Gesso
Delta Ceramcoat All Purpose Sealer
Delta Ceramcoat Gloss Interior
    Varnish
Chacopaper

Sources

Refer to page 44.

PREPARATION

1. Please read carefully the General Instructions on pages 2-3 before starting this project. Pattern is on page 23.
2. Sand the wood lightly, then seal with a wood sealer. Once the wood has dried thoroughly, sand it again for a smooth finish. If there are imperfections in the wood beyond what sanding will repair, use a paintable wood filler to fix it, and then sand again.

BASECOATING

1. It is likely that you will need more than one coat of each color for complete coverage. I recommend two to three thin coats, rather than one thick coat that may be uneven and difficult to paint over.
2. Use the ¾" wash for the larger sections and the #14 flat for narrower areas and touch up.
3. Paint the underside of the stool top with Copen Blue.
4. Transfer just the center circle to the top of the stool using *Chacopaper*. You will need the full design later.
5. **Top:** Using the #12 round brush and Bright Yellow, paint the daisy center. Using the ¾" flat wash brush and a mix of Copen Blue + Pthalo Blue (1:1), paint the remainder of the top, extending the color to cover the edge of the seat.
6. **Legs:** Paint the bottom and top sections of each leg in Fuchsia and the center section in Pumpkin.

PAINTING THE DESIGN
Stool Top

1. Transfer the full flower design to the top of the stool.
2. With the ½" filbert brush and white gesso, paint the basic shape of the petals. Start from the outside painting towards the center, and allow your strokes to enter the center circle. You will paint over this again.
3. When the gesso is dry, paint over the petals using Ivory and the ½" filbert.
4. With the ½" flat comb, drybrush white over petals at each end (center of flower and tip of petal.)
5. With the #14 flat and thinned paint, float shading on random petals. This will differentiate some petals in front of others. So, you may have one petal that is behind the petals on either side of it (in which case, you would shade both sides of the petal), and others might dip behind another on just one side. Some petals will be entirely above the petals on either side of it.
6. Start with floating thinned Fuchsia (thin about 60% with water) and shade the base of every petal in a "U" shape where it meets the center. Then shade the sides of petals as you choose (or look at the photo for guidance).
7. When the Fuchsia paint is dry, paint Pumpkin on alternate petals and at the tips of some petals.
8. Using the #12 round, paint the center with Bright Yellow. Use as many coats as needed to cover any white

This jazzy stool is great for preschoolers to tweens. The bold design and bright colors make it a fun spot to sit down to read a book or rest during playtime.

that has been painted over it. Allow to dry.

9. With the #14 flat and Pumpkin (thinned 50% with water), float shading-color around the entire inside perimeter of the yellow center. Allow to dry, and then shade one side of the center with a wider band of color.

10. With the ½" flat comb, wash Lima Green (thinned 50% with water) on the center of each petal and on the flower center.

11. With the ½" flat comb, drybrush Copen Blue (thinned 50% with water) from the center of the flower outward on each petal.

12. With the #2 liner and Pumpkin, paint a wavy line around the center of the flower.

Note: Load your liner brush with a paint/water mixture in an ink-like consistency. Keep your brush handle perpendicular to your surface at all times and use only the tip of the brush! Don't worry about making the lines perfectly straight. Mine aren't!

13. With the handle of a small brush (such as a liner), add dots to the center using Pumpkin (see photo). Add more dots using a mix of Pumpkin + Ivory (1:1), working from the outside towards the center. Clean the handle, and then add dots with Crocus Yellow (just a few) at the very center. Be sure to let handle dots dry well before you work over the area, as they will drip or smear if not fully dry.

14. With the #14 flat, float Pthalo Blue around the outside edges of the flower petals on the blue background.

15. With the #1 liner, add a series of wavy lines around the outside of each petal (see note in step 12). Start with Magnolia White. Clean the brush, and then add wavy lines with Crocus Yellow. To each petal, add one or two "V" shaped crease lines where the petal meets the center of the flower. Add a final set of wavy lines around the petals with Fuchsia (thinned 80% with water.)

Side Edge & Legs

1. Around the outside edge of the top of the stool add handle dots with Lima Green. Allow to dry well.

2. Add Pumpkin handle dots to the top Fuchsia section of each leg; add Lima Green dots to the bottom Fuchsia section.

3. Using the #2 liner brush, add a band of Copen Blue at the bottom of each Pumpkin section and around the groove near the top of the section.

4. Paint the swirl design freehand using a liner brush. (See illustrations on page 22.) Paint swirls in a chain.

Each new swirl starts on the curve of the swirl before it. Vary the size and direction of the swirls as you paint them for more visual interest. If you prefer, you can paint a small comma stroke at the end of each swirl to give it a "capped" effect.

FINISHING

1. When all paint has dried, varnish with at least three coats of *Delta Ceramcoat Gloss Interior Varnish*.

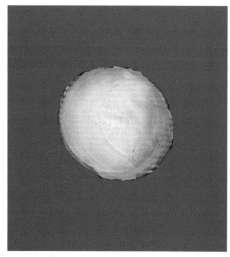

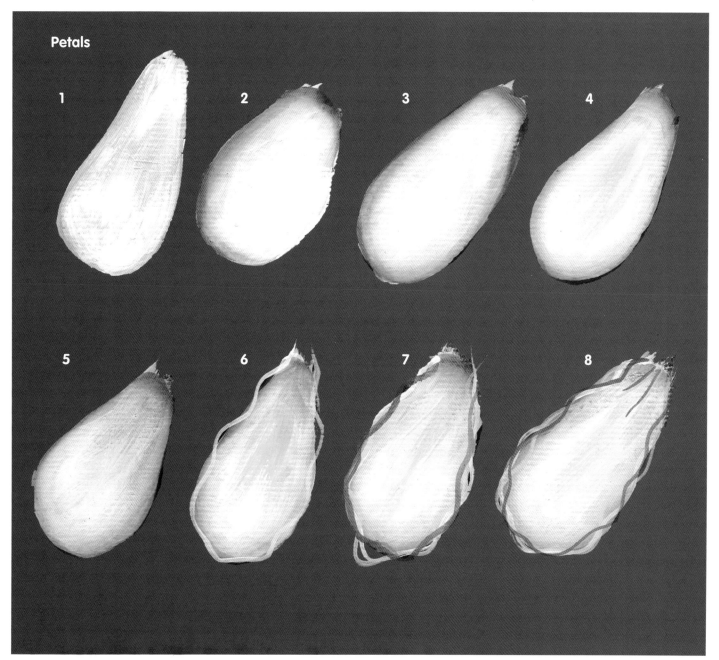

Petals

1   2   3   4

5   6   7   8

Sailor's Footlocker

By Deb Malewski

Palette

DecoArt Americana Acrylics
Admiral Blue
Baby Blue
Bittersweet Chocolate
Country Red
French Vanilla
Glorious Gold
Golden Straw
Honey Brown
Fiery Red (Hot Shots)
Lamp Black
Light Cinnamon
Payne's Grey
Sapphire Blue
Titanium White

Brushes

Royal & Langnickel
10/0 round (Fusion): Series 3250
#14 round (Royal Sable): Series 5005
#8, 10 shaders (Fusion): Series 3150
⅜" filbert (Aqualon Wisp): Series 2935
½" stencil brush (Crafter's Choice): R9111

Surface

Wood flip-top stool, 9½"H x 13"W
    x 9"D (#137-9185) available from
    Viking Woodcrafts.

Other Supplies

Decoart Americana Sealer
Decoart Americana Matte Varnish

Sources

Refer to page 44.

PREPARATION & BACKGROUND

1. Please read carefully the General Instructions on pages 2-3 before starting this project. Patterns are on the center insert.

2. Seal the stool and sand. Basecoat with Admiral Blue.

3. Using the #14 round brush, pick up Sapphire Blue, scrub most of the paint off on a paper towel, then scrub the surfaces in a circular, random pattern.

4. Repeat using Baby Blue. This will create a mottled look to the background. Using the stencil brush and Baby Blue, flyspeck the surface.

5. Apply the pattern.

STOOL TOP

1. **Flag stripes:** Paint alternate stripes Titanium White, shaded with Admiral Blue, and Country Red, shaded with Lamp Black and highlighted with Hot Shots Fiery Red. Using the ⅜" filbert wisp brush, add texture lines on white stripes with Admiral Blue and on red areas with Lamp Black. Use the wisp to drybrush the shading for a soft look.

2. **Star field:** Use Sapphire Blue shaded on the side and bottom edges with Admiral Blue. Highlight in the center by drybrushing using the wisp brush and Baby Blue.

3. **Flag pole:** Attach flag to pole with Titanium White "strings" around the pole. Stars are Titanium White. Flag pole is Light Cinnamon, shaded at each end with Bittersweet Chocolate and lightly highlighted with Golden Straw. Top of the flag pole is Golden Straw, shaded with Honey Brown and then Light Cinnamon. Add Titanium White highlights. Titanium White stars are on Titanium White strings, with

Sapphire, Titanium White, and Country Red beads.

4. **Shirt:** Paint with Admiral Blue, shade with Payne's Grey, and highlight with Sapphire, then Baby Blue. Using the wisp brush and Baby Blue, drybrush more highlights on the collar and sleeves. Lines on collar and sleeves and the bow are Titanium White. The shirt dickey is Titanium White, shaded with Admiral Blue. Add Admiral Blue stripes on the dickey. Line the shirt with Sapphire Blue to help it stand out from the background.

5. **Sand:** Using the stencil brush and Honey Brown, pounce the sand on. Pick up a small amount of Titanium White and continue pouncing.

6. **Water:** Wisp on water at left side using Sapphire Blue and the wisp. Pick up some Titanium White and pounce the white water breaking on the sand.

7. **Bear head, hands, and legs:** Using the dampened wisp brush and Honey Brown, basecoat the bear parts. Pick up the paint in the brush, and spread it for the head, working in a circle and pulling from the center out. This makes the edges wispier. (see worksheet on page 31.) Fill in the head completely, then add two half circles for the ears, again pulling out from the head. Add a bit of hair on the chest area.

Without cleaning your brush and without letting the Honey Brown dry, pick up some Golden Straw in your wisp and add strokes to highlight the head. Again, work in a circle, pulling from the center out. Highlight the tops of the ears. Pick up more Golden Straw and paint the muzzle, once

Ahoy mates! This red, white, and blue stool will inspire dreams of sailing the high seas. The lid opens to provide a handy place for stashing treasures.

again working in a circle and pulling from the center out.

Paint the hands and legs using the same technique. Base the areas with Honey Brown, using the wisp, and then add highlights of Golden Straw. Add more highlights of French Vanilla to all fur areas using the wisp. Add French Vanilla highlights to the top of the ears, tops of the muzzle, and to the head, chest, hands, and legs. Using the wisp brush, pick up Light Cinnamon and pat it in the center of the ears for shading. Pat short strokes around the muzzle to shade and to make it stand out from the head. Shade under the chin, at wrists, and between legs and feet just by patting short strokes of the Light Cinnamon. When that is dry, use the shader brush and Light Cinnamon to intensify the shading with the traditional sideload method. Shade around the muzzle then flip the brush over and shade on the bottom of the muzzle. Shade the wrists, between the legs and between the feet. Using the shader brush and Bittersweet Chocolate, shade in the top part of each ear. Using the wisp and French Vanilla, pull a few more strokes of hair over the shading to soften it.

8. **Facial features:** Add features with Bittersweet Chocolate and the 10/0 round brush. Use Titanium White to highlight the nose then add a white dot in the upper right of each eye. Blush cheeks using the #14 round brush and Country Red. Pick up a small amount of Country Red in your brush and scrub most of it off on your paper towel. With a very light touch, rub the cheeks; it's easier to add more if it's too light than to take it off! Freckles are Light Cinnamon made with the round brush so that they aren't perfectly round. Bottom lip is French Vanilla made with the round brush. Inside the mouth is Bittersweet Chocolate. Shade under the nose and lips with Light Cinnamon using the shader brush. Highlight the top lip by lightly floating French Vanilla.

9. **Hat:** Base Titanium White; shade with Admiral Blue. The star is Country Red with Titanium White line work.

SIDES OF BOX

1. **Edge of lid:** I took Baby Blue on my wisp brush and just wisped down on each edge of the lid, creating lots of little lines.

2. Apply the pattern to one end, then reverse it for the other end. The chain and charms should be at the back of the box.

3. Paint the compass face with Titanium White and shade with Admiral Blue. Line work is Lamp Black. The compass rose is Lamp Black with Glorious Gold circles in the center. The case is Glorious Gold with Titanium White highlights at about 2 o'clock and 8 o'clock. Line gold areas with Lamp Black.

3. Beads and chain are Glorious Gold, highlighted with Titanium White and lined with Lamp Black.

4. Star charms are Country Red (lined with Glorious Gold), Snow White (shaded with Admiral Blue at the bottom), and Sapphire (lined with Baby Blue). Flag is Sapphire, lined with Baby Blue and Titanium star. Stripes are Titanium White and Country Red. Shade white areas with Admiral Blue.

5. Shade behind compass, beads, stars, and flag with Payne's Grey using the shader brush.

FRONT OF BOX

1. The rope is Titanium White, shaded with Admiral Blue.

2. Bears are both painted the same. Using the wisp brush and Honey Brown, work in a circle, pulling from the center out. Add ears the same way. Pick up Golden Straw with the wisp and add highlights to fur, again pulling from the center out. Pick up more Golden Straw and add muzzle. Still using the wisp, pick up Light Cinnamon and pat in ears and around muzzle to

30

shade. Paint a few hairs at the base of each ear to shade. When dry, pick up the shader brush and Light Cinnamon, and shade in the traditional sideload method around the muzzle. Using the shader brush, pick up Bittersweet Chocolate and shade the inside top of each ear. Using the wisp brush, pick up French Vanilla and add more highlights to head and ears.

3. Using the round brush and Bittersweet Chocolate, paint facial features. Add highlights with Titanium White. Freckles are Light Cinnamon made with the round brush. Checks are blushed with Country Red, using the #14 round brush and gently scrubbing the color on. Using the round brush and French Vanilla, paint the lower lip. When dry, shade under the nose and lips with Light Cinnamon using the shader brush. Highlight the top lip with French Vanilla using the shader brush.

4. The sailor boy hat and bow are Titanium White, shaded with Admiral Blue. The star is Country Red with Titanium White line work.

5. The sailor girl's hair bow is Sapphire, shaded with Admiral Blue and highlighted with Baby Blue. Stars are Titanium White. The collar is Admiral Blue, highlighted with Baby Blue. The line for the trim is Titanium White. The dickey is Titanium White, shaded with Admiral Blue and with Country Red stripes. The bow is Country Red, shaded with Lamp Black and highlighted with Hot Shots Fiery Red.

6. If needed, pull a few strokes of French Vanilla using the wisp brush to add more hair over shaded areas and clothes.

FINISHING

Varnish with several coats of matte varnish.

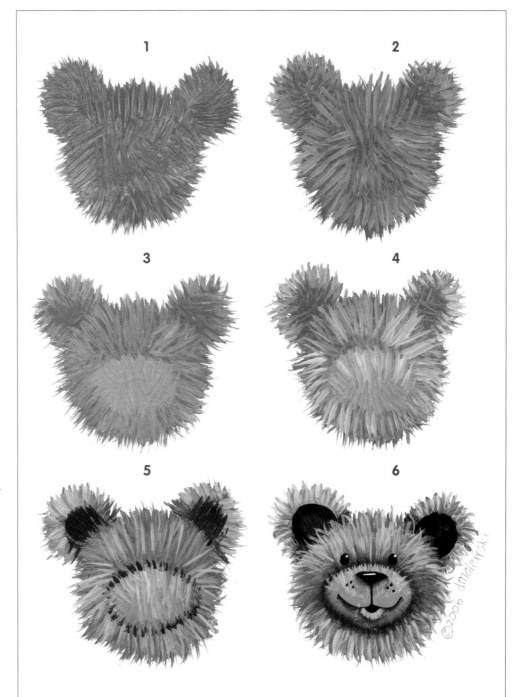

PAINTING THE BEAR

Step 1. Basecoat using dampened Wisp brush, pulling from center out.

Step 2. Whitout cleaning brush and without letting first coat dry, use Wisp to apply highllights; again, pull from center out.

Step 3. Using wisp brush add muzzle, pulling from center out.

Step 4. Using Wisp brush and second highlight color, add more highlights.

Step 5. Clean Wisp brush. Using shading color, pat brush in base of ears and around muzzle to create shading.

Step 6. Using #8 shader brush and Bittersweet Chocolate, shade tops of ears. Using same brush and light Cinnamon, shade around muzzle, on the bottom of the muzzle. under nose, and under lips.

By Chris Thornton

ABC Come Read with Me

Palette

Delta Creative Ceramcoat® Acrylics

Black
Crocus Yellow
Deep Lilac
Denim Blue
Fuchsia
Hunter Green
Laguna Blue
Lime Green
Mulberry
Navy Blue
Persimmon
Purple
Raw Sienna
Tomato Spice
White

Brushes

Loew-Cornell, La Corneille Golden Taklon

#0 script liner: Series 7050
#6, 10, 12 shaders: Series 7300
#2 round stroke: Series 7040
1" wash: Series 7350

Surface

Bench, 10½"H x 25"W x 10½"D, wood butterfly cutout and letters all purchased from the craft store.

Other Supplies

Delta Creative Ceramcoat® Brush Cleaner
Delta Creative Ceramcoat® Faux Glaze Medium Clear
Delta Creative Ceramcoat® Satin Exterior/Interior Varnish
Delta Creative Ceramcoat® All-Purpose Sealer
Seawool sponge
Old toothbrush
Sharpie Fine-Point Black Permanent Marker (new)
Wood glue

Sources

Refer to page 44.

PREPARATION & BACKGROUND

1. Please read carefully the General Instructions on pages 2-3 before starting this project. Patterns are on the center insert and pages 30-31.
2. Apply an even coat of all-purpose sealer to all pieces using the 1" wash brush; allow to dry then sand.
3. Basecoat the entire bench in Denim Blue using the 1" wash brush.
4. *Mix Faux Glaze Medium + Navy Blue (2:1).* Using a seawool sponge, pat into the mix then pat excess off on your palette. Pat on bench, randomly working one area at a time. Rotate the sponge to the clean side and soften edges of dark blue. Repeat the process until all of bench is covered.
5. Spatter here and there in main sections using an old toothbrush and White.
6. Line the bench seat, backrest, and outside each side piece using Crocus Yellow and the #1 liner.
7. Apply the patterns for the bugs, flowers, and lettering randomly as desired (see photo for ideas). If your little reader has a favorite bug you may choose to use only that bug.

PAINTING THE DESIGN

1. Basecoat butterflies using Crocus Yellow and the #12 shader; use Crocus Yellow and the #6 shader for the lettering and bee's bodies. Float shadows with Raw Sienna using the same brush (see worksheet on page 35). Float highlights with White + a touch of Crocus Yellow using the same brush.
2. Basecoat the dragonfly wings, leaves, "C", and hearts on butterfly Lime Green using an appropriate sized brush. Float shadows Hunter Green and highlights White + a touch of Lime Green.
3. Basecoat letters "A" and "M", ladybug, and hearts on butterfly wings in Fuchsia. Float Mulberry shadows and use White + a touch of Fuchsia for the highlights.
4. Basecoat one flower and the heart on the butterfly wing using Persimmon and the #10 shader. Float Tomato Spice shadows and highlight with White + a touch of Persimmon using same brush.
5. Basecoat one flower, letters "B" and "E", the bee's wings and heart on the butterfly wing in Laguna Blue using appropriate sized brush. Float Navy Blue shadows and highlight with White + a touch of Laguna using same brush.
6. Basecoat the edge of butterflies, one flower, and hearts on dragonfly wings using Deep Lilac and appropriate sized brush. Float Purple shadows and highlight with White + a touch of Deep Lilac.
7. Paint centers of flowers with Crocus Yellow; float shadows with Raw Sienna and highlights with White + a touch of Crocus Yellow.
8. Paint all bug bodies (including antennae) using Black and appropriate sized brush. Float highlights with White + a touch of Deep Lilac. Highlight the antennae with a line of the same color.
9. Use the large end of a stylus and Persimmon to dot the end of the antennae.
10. Add large and small dots on ladybugs using Black and the stylus and also add dots around centers of flowers.

There's room for two on this colorful bench where whimsical butterflies, bees, and bugs beckon little tykes to enjoy reading their favorite books.

FINISHING

1. Use a black permanent marking pen for outlining. Outline letters just inside the edge, breaking the line occasionally for variety. Outline the letters for the words then add loose shadow outlines (about 1/16" from first line) as desired. Outline flowers in the same way and add a vein line in the middle of each leaf. Outline bugs in the same way and add more lines on wings to define heart shapes (see photo and worksheet).

2. Use the liner brush and White to add the curly dashed lines for the ladybug trails, filling in blank areas.

3. Glue letters and butterfly in place.

4. Apply as many coats of satin exterior/interior varnish as desired using the 1" glaze brush.

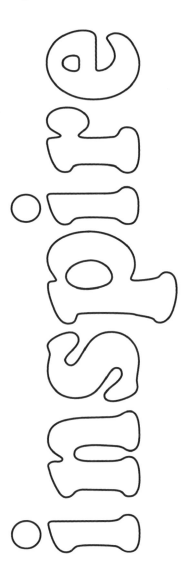

with

read

dream
grow
come

35

Magical Blooms

By Julia Minasian

Palette

Delta Ceramcoat Acrylics
Fire Red
Lilac Dusk
Metallic Kim Gold "Gleams"
Pumpkin
FolkArt Acrylic Colors
French Vanilla
Fresh Foliage

Brushes

Loew-Cornell, Inc.
#1, 3 rounds: Series 3000

Surface

Child's rocking chair with dark finish,
28"H x 16"W x 13"D,
purchased from thrift store.

Other Supplies

*Design Master Super Surface Spray
Sealer, Satin*
Loew-Cornell White Transfer Paper
Ribbon to match color palette

Sources

Refer to page 44.

PREPARATION

1. Please read carefully the General Instructions on pages 2-3 before starting this project. Patterns are on pages 38-39.
2. Be sure your prefinished chair is clean and free of dust before painting your design.
3. Trace the pattern and transfer to the chair areas as shown in the photo or make copies of the design elements and arrange them to fit your particular chair. If you like, you can wrap some of the icons around to the back of the chair.

PAINTING THE DESIGN

1. Paint the largest areas of color using the #3 round and small areas with the #1 round. You may want more than one coat if you like a solid look. I allowed parts of the wood to show through so that I could use the dark wood for added dimension and give an illusion of flower veins. It is important to paint each petal or leaf from either the outside towards the center or vice versa. Make smaller petals using just one or two strokes.
2. While you have the different colors on your brush, when painting the assorted flowers, you may want to paint the bands of color along the chair rung as well as circles for the polka dots on the arms.

Hibiscus on Seat

1. Paint the leaf with Fresh Foliage and the flower petals with Lilac Dusk. For a painterly look, allow some of the dark wood to show through rather than covering opaquely.

2. Paint the flower center and stamen using Fire Red. Shade the petals with long slightly curved strokes of Fire Red pulled from the outside edges (see photo).
3. Using the #1 round, paint squiggly lines in the center first with FrenchVanilla then with Pumpkin and Metallic Kim Gold. Use the same colors to add accent outlines on the edges of the petals.
4. Use the end of the brush to add Pumpkin dots just outside the center with a few placed randomly on the petals.
5. Add a few French Vanilla dots and dot the length of the stamen with French Vanilla.
6. Paint dabs of color on the anthers at the ends of the stamen using Fresh Foliage, Pumpkin, French Vanilla, and Metallic Kim Gold.
7. Outline the leaf and paint dots using French Vanilla. Highlight dots with "C" strokes of Metallic Kim Gold on the left side and add a stroke of gold along the bottom edge of the leaf.

Backrest Flowers

1. Refer to the pattern and key for placement of basecoat colors.
2. Use the #1 round for the detail dots and strokes. Use small amounts of paint on just the tip of the brush to make these dot points.
3. For the large Lilac 5-petal flower, dot around the edge of two petals using Fresh Foliage, then dot the remaining petals using French Vanilla, Pumpkin and Fire Red. Dot the petals and the lower left leaf with French Vanilla.
4. Dot the centers of the small Lilac 5-petal flowers with four tiny dots of

French Vanilla on one side and a large Pumpkin dot on the other.

5. For the Lilac tulip, add Fire Red dots inside the curved edge and a row of dots down the center. Also place four dots just below the blossom.

6. For the Pumpkin tulip stripe the outside petals and dot the center petal using Fire Red then outline petal edges with tiny dots of French Vanilla.

7. Accent leaves with splashes of metallic Kim Gold and French Vanilla for the finishing touch. Follow the flow of each shape and put touches here and there. Don't overdo it!

Stripes & Dots

1. Use all the colors from your palette for the dots on the armrests and color bands on the chair rung. The overall feel of this design is loose, so make your color placement random. The dots should be unevenly spaced and different sizes. As you place each dot, if you think of the three points of a triangle, it will help you to maintain a random look but with a "roughly" even flow. See the illustration on page 40 for an example.

2. Color bands should also vary in size and placement. I used the natural wood as a color, leaving a couple of unpainted bands.

FINISHING

1. It is always nice to paint your name and the date somewhere inconspicuously like underneath the chair seat.

2. When the paint is dry, apply a thin coat of spray sealer for protection.

3. Once the sealer is dry, tie a couple of pretty bows to the arms to bring a little textural bounce.

Make an old rocker new with this delightful medley of dots, stripes, and fantasy flowers. And can you believe they're painted using just six colors?

Dot placement
sample

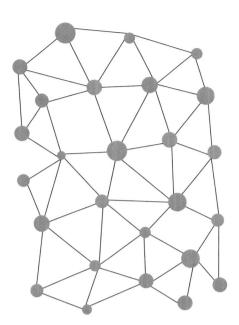

Backrest Pattern
actual size

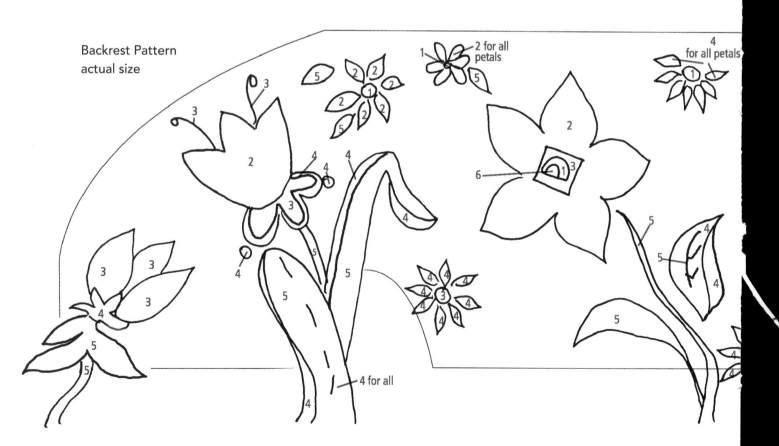

2 for all
petals

4
for all petals

4 for all

38

1. Fire Red
2. Lilac Dusk
3. Pumpkin
4. French Vanilla
5. Fresh Foliage
6. Metallic Kim Gold

Seat Pattern
Enlarge 200% for
actual size

Armrest Heart
Pattern
actual size

4 for all petals

39

Dance, Ballerina, Dance

By Deb Malewski

Palette
DecoArt Americana Acrylics
Baby Pink
Bittersweet Chocolate
Boysenberry
Dark Hauser Green
French Vanilla
Golden Straw
Honey Brown
Light Cinnamon
Light Hauser Green
Titanium White

Brushes
Royal & Langnickel
10/0 round *(Fusion)*: Series 3250
#14 round *(Royal Sable)*: Series
   5005
#8, 10 shaders *(Fusion)*: Series 3150
⅜" filbert *(Aqualon Wisp)*: Series
   2935
½" stencil brush *(Crafter's Choice)*:
   R9111

Surface
Wooden chair, 26"H x 12"W x
   11"D, (#22) available from
   LittleColorado.com.

Other Supplies
Masking tape
Star stencil (optional)
Decoart Americana Wood Sealer
Decoart Americana Matte Varnish

Sources
Refer to page 44.

PREPARATION & BACKGROUND
1. Please read carefully the General Instructions on pages 2-3 before starting this project. Patterns are on page 43 and the center insert.
2. Seal the chair and sand. Basecoat the back and seat in Baby Pink and the leg and base areas in Titanium White.
3. For the background effect in the pink areas, load the #14 round brush with some Boysenberry, scrub most of it off on paper towels, then "scrub" onto the surface in a circular motion in random areas. It will look a bit mottled. Repeat this method using Titanium White.
4. Fly speck using Boysenberry and the stencil brush then add more fly specking using Titanium White. See step by step samples on page 43.
5. Use masking tape to create the stripes on the bottom areas of the chair. Leave about a tape-width between each strip of tape. Work in one area at a time before moving to another section, re-using tape strips as you move around the chair. Using the stencil brush, apply Baby Pink between the strips of tape.
6. When dry lightly pounce a bit of Boysenberry at the bottom of each stripe. Let dry then use the #14 round to dry brush Titanium White in the middle of each stripe. Use your finger to blend the edges of the White, if needed.
7. Flyspeck the White area with Boysenberry using the stencil brush.
8. Transfer the main parts of the design to the chair.

PAINTING THE DESIGN
Chair Seat
1. The ribbon on the bow continues down each side of the chair. Paint it Baby Pink, shade with Boysenberry, and highlight with Snow White + Baby Pink. Shade and highlight several times to achieve depth in your shading.
2. Using the #14 round brush and Titanium White, add more highlights to the bow by dry brushing in the center of the knot, on the top and bottom of the loops, on the cut ends, and down the center length of the ribbon wrapping around. Again, repeat this several times to get a nice white highlight against the pink.
3. Using the 10/0 round brush and Boysenberry, add thin lines on the ribbon. Using Titanium White, line all edges of the ribbon.

Backrest
1. The lettering is Baby Pink, shaded with Boysenberry and highlighted with Baby Pink + Titanium White. Repeat shading and highlighting several times to get good depth.
2. Outline each letter with Titanium White. Shade around each letter with Boysenberry.

Tutu/Leotard
1. Paint the leotard before you paint the bear, but not the skirt. The skirt will be added after the bear is painted. The leotard is Titanium White, shaded with Boysenberry around the edges.
2. To create the belt just shade above and below the area, and then add more Boysenberry shading at the sides.

3. Add more center highlights to the leotard using the #14 round brush and Titanium White and dry brushing.

4. The rose is just a circle of Boysenberry with strokes of Titanium White added to make the petals. Paint the leaves Hauser Light Green and shade and line them with Hauser Dark Green.

Bear

1. Paint the bear using the dampened ⅜" filbert wisp brush. Start by picking up Honey Brown and working in a circle for the head, pulling the brush from the center out, so that the strokes are wispiest at the edges (see bear worksheet on page 31). Fill in the circle completely then add two half-circles the same way for the ears.

2. Before the paint dries and without cleaning your brush, pick up Golden Straw and use the same technique (pulling from the center to the edges) to lightly add highlights. You want to still be able to see the background color.

3. Picking up more Golden Straw in your brush, paint the muzzle. Work in a circle, pulling from the center out in an oval shape. Still without cleaning your brush, pick up French Vanilla and add more highlights to the head and top of the muzzle.

4. Clean your wisp brush and pick up some Light Cinnamon for shading. Pat the Light Cinnamon in the ears, adding a few strokes at the base of the ears, also. Shade the muzzle by patting short strokes of the Light Cinnamon around the muzzle so that it appears to stand out from the head.

Your little ballerina will love taking a break from pirouettes with her bear friend on this so girly pink chair.

Boysenberry, shade under each layer.

11. Face details: Eyes, nose and mouth are Bittersweet Chocolate. Highlight eyes and nose with a Titanium White. Inside mouth area is also Bittersweet Chocolate. Use the liner brush and French Vanilla to paint the bottom lip. Add freckles with a stylus and Light Cinnamon. Blush cheeks using the #14 round brush and Boysenberry. Pick up paint in the brush, scrub most of it off on a paper towel, then gently rub the cheek area. It's easier to add more than to try to take it off, so start out lightly.

12. Hair bow: Bow is Baby Pink, shaded with Boysenberry and highlighted with Baby Pink + Titanium White. Line with Titanium White. Shade under the bow on the fur with Light Cinnamon using the shader brush.

13. Intensify all Light Cinnamon shaded areas using the shader brush. Shade under the tutu skirt where it goes over the legs. Shade around the muzzle with Light Cinnamon with a somewhat "shaky" hand to preserve some of the wispiness, and then flip the brush and shade the bottom of the actual muzzle. Shade under the nose and under the lips with Light Cinnamon using the shader brush.

14. Using the 10/0 liner brush and French Vanilla, add more hair to the bear. Curve the srands more at this step and add them in small groups of three or so. Add a group curving to the right, then some to the left so that it looks natural.

15. Stars are Titanium White. If you prefer, use a stencil rather than transferring them from the pattern. Dots are Titanium White made with the stylus. Add a hazy effect by scrubbing Titanium White around them with the #14 round brush.

FINISHING

1. Varnish with several coats of matte varnish.

You will be doing more shading later to intensify it.

5. Fill in the chest area with Honey Brown using the wisp brush, then add a few strokes of Golden Straw to highlight, pulling down. Shade under the chin with the wisp and Light Cinnamon by pulling down a few short strokes.

6. Paint the arms with Honey Brown and the wisp brush, with strokes of Golden Straw pulling up and gently curving. Add more highlights of French Vanilla. Shade at the base of the arms using the wisp and Light Cinnamon

7. Paint legs the same as the arms, pulling the highlights down and gently curving. Shade at the top and bottom with short strokes of Light Cinnamon.

8. Ballet shoes and ribbons are Titanium White, shaded with Boysenberry.

9. Roses are Boysenberry, with strokes of Titanium White for petals. Leaves are Hauser Light Green and are lined with Hauser Dark Green.

10. Tutu skirt: Sideload the #10 shader with Titanium White. Start at the side and pull down, creating a Titanium White edge but a sheer center. Work across with the sideloaded brush in scallops. Add more layers. Using the wisp brush and Titanium White, pull lines down the tutu skirt. Using the shader brush and

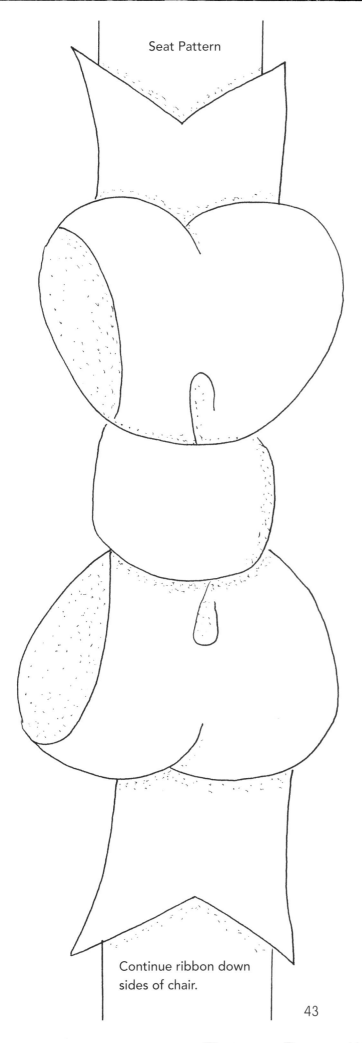

Seat Pattern

Continue ribbon down sides of chair.

1. Basecoat with Baby Pink. Pick up Boysenberry in the sable brush. Scrub most of it off on your paper towel, then gently scrub the painting surface.

2. Repeat using a bit of Titanium White in the sable brush. The surface will look mottled.

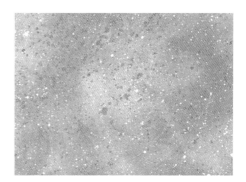

3. Using a stencil brush, pick up Titanium White and flyspeck the surface. To flyspeck, slightly thin your paint, and fill your stencil brush with it. Using a brush handle or dowel, pull the bristles of the brush *towards* you as you hold the brush parallel to the surface. The paint should flick away from you. Repeat using Boysenberry. Let dry well, as the dots of paint will take a bit longer to dry.

Artists

Gillum, Linda
Kooler Design Studio
399 Taylor Blvd., #104
Pleasant Hill, CA 94523
925-689-0801
www.koolerdesign.com

Harris, Peggy
3848 Martin's Chapel Rd.
Springfield, TN 37172
615-382-2050
peggy@peggyharris.com
www.peggyharris.com

Hillman, Barbara Baatz
6 Lake St.
Pittsburg, CA 94565
925-432-4971
baatzbf@aol.com

Leigh, Tera
7063 Montanes Ln.
Carlsbad, CA 92009
tera@teraleigh.com
www.teraleigh.com

Malewski, Deb
1308 Hall St.
Eaton Rapids, MI 48827
517-256-9460
debmalewski@sbcglobal.net
www.debmalewski.com

Minasian, Julia
925-943-1047
juliaminasian@sbcglobal.net
www.juliamdesign.com

Thornton, Chris
P.O. Box 617
Douglass, KS 67039
316-253-5442
cricinda@earthllink.net

Sources

Cabin Crafters
P.O. Box 270
Nevada, IA 50201
800-689-3920
www.cabincrafters.com

DecoArt, Inc.
P.O. Box 386
Stanford, KY 40484
606-365-3193
www.decoart.com

Delta Ceramcoat
Delta Technical Coatings
2690 Pellissier Pl.
City of Industry, CA 90601
800-423-4135
www.deltacrafts.com

Design Master
P.O. Box 601
Boulder, CO 80306-0601
303-443-5214
www.dmcolor.com

FolkArt
Plaid Enterprises, Inc.
P.O. Box 7600
Norcross, GA 30091
770-923-8200
www.plaidonline.com

J.W., etc.
11972 Hertz St.
Moorpark, CA 93021
805-529-9500
www.jwetc.com

Little Colorado, Inc.
(303) 964-3212
www.littlecolorado.com

Loew-Cornell, Inc.
400 Sylvan Ave.
Englewood Cliffs, NJ 07632
201-836-7070
www.loew-cornell.com

Masterson's Sta-Wet Palette
P.O. Box 11301
Phoenix, AZ 85017
800-965-2675
www.mastersonart.com

Peggy's Ultimate Varnish Brush
See Peggy Harris at left.

Robert Simmons Brushes
Daler-Rowney U.S.A., Ltd.
2 Corporate Dr.
Cranburry, NJ 08512-9584
609-655-5252
www.daler-rowney.com

Royal & Langnickel
Royal Brush Manufacturing
6707 Broadway
Merrillville, IN 46410
800-247-2211
www.royalbrush.com

Silver Brush Limited
P.O. Box 414
Windsor, NJ 08561-0414
www.silverbrush.com

Viking Woodcrafts, Inc.
1317 8th St. SE,
Waseca, MN 56093
800-328-0116
www.vikingwoodcrafts.com

Produced by:
Kooler Design Studio
399 Taylor Blvd., Ste. 104
Pleasant Hill, CA 94523
kds@koolerdesign.com

- Creative Director, Donna Kooler
- Editor-in-Chief, Judy Swager
- Graphic Designer, María A. Parrish
- Proofreader, Char Randolph
- Photographer, Dianne Woods
- Photo Stylist, Basha Kooler

Published by:

the art of everyday living

Copyright ©2006 by Leisure Arts, Inc.
5701 Ranch Drive, Little Rock, AR 72223
www.leisurearts.com
ISBN 1-60140-427-1